To Rosen

Y.

Love/you x
2015

PORTRAIT OF
CANTERBURY

ANDREAS BYRNE

HALSGROVE

First published in Great Britain in 2008

British Library Cataloguing-in-Publication Data
A CIP record for this title is available from the British Library

ISBN 978 1 84114 767 3

HALSGROVE
Halsgrove House
Ryelands Industrial Estate
Bagley Road, Wellington, Somerset TA21 9PZ
Tel: 01823 653777   Fax: 01823 216796
email: sales@halsgrove.com
website: www.halsgrove.com

Printed and bound by
D'Auria Industrie Grafiche, Italy

INTRODUCTION

Portrait of Canterbury is a photographic journey through the city of Canterbury and the surrounding area. I have used the postcode area of Canterbury as my guide, encompassing beautiful Kentish villages, castles, windmills, marshes and white weather-boarded houses. To the north and west of Canterbury is the ancient woodland of Blean which is the most extensive in the south. Dominating the landscape is the magnificent cathedral and all the history that goes with it, particularly the murder of Thomas Becket in 1170. The cathedral has welcomed pilgrims from all over the world and there is a walk in Kent known as the Pilgrims Way that leads to Canterbury from London. The city of Canterbury offers so much to me as the photographer, from the modern Marlow Theatre to the ancient Westgate Towers. It has an intriguing maze of narrow cobbled streets dotted with medieval timbered buildings, some at very strange angles! The River Stour runs through the city reflecting buildings and bridges as it flows. The stunning medieval Gothic architecture of the cathedral glows golden in the low evening sunlight and is magnificent. I was astounded by the giant columns and arches inside the cathedral, the functional and yet beautiful bones that support the great weight of the central tower. When sunlight pours through the delicate medieval stained glass windows they light up in a rainbow of colours and are a joy to behold, (don't fancy the job of cleaning them though!).

The surrounding villages and towns are a mix of charming, picturesque and quaint buildings, many of the houses dating from medieval times. They nestle in the valleys of the Kent Downs Area of Outstanding Natural Beauty and retain their tranquillity in spite of the proximity of motorways and the Channel Tunnel Rail Link. Each village has an ancient church steeped in history, olde worlde pubs, village greens and a network of way-marked cycle and footpaths from which to enjoy the countryside. The footpaths have wonderful names, such as The Crab & Winkle Way leading from Canterbury to Whitstable, Saxon Shore Way which is a coastal route and numerous valley walks which often follow rivers showing off Kent's prettiest and most outstanding views. Kent is surely still 'The Garden of England', and Canterbury the jewel at its heart.

ACKNOWLEDGEMENTS

I would like to thank Canterbury Cathedral and English Heritage for allowing me to use the photographs taken on their properties.

I would also like to thank Juliette Nicholson for her beautiful illustrated map used in *Portrait of Canterbury.*

LOCATION MAP – Canterbury

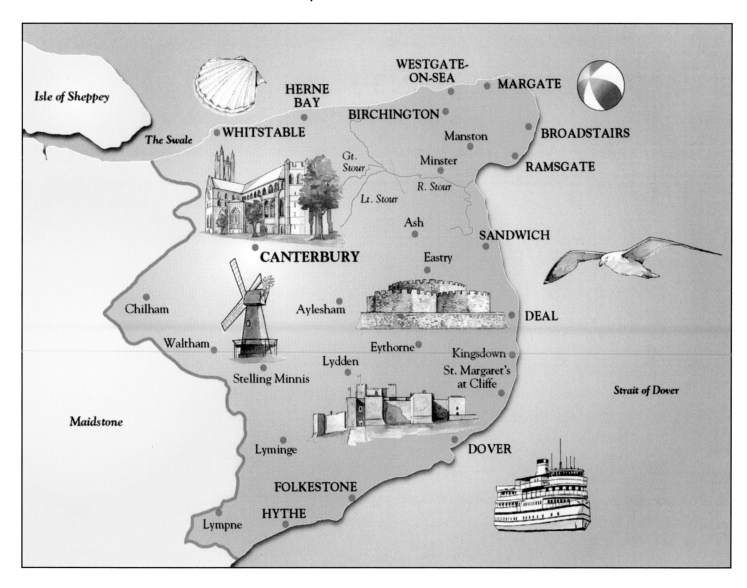

Canterbury Cathedral at dusk. The floodlit cathedral, which history dates back to 597AD, glows golden against the dusky blue twilight sky.

Marlowe Theatre.
The Marlowe Theatre is the largest in Kent and hosts shows all year round. The theatre was named after one of Canterbury's most famous sons, Christopher Marlowe (1564–93) a famous playwright. Christopher Marlowe was educated at King's School, Canterbury.

Opposite:
The metal sculpture mask.
The metal sculpture mask sits outside the Marlowe Theatre.

Havelock Street.
The cathedral tower stands high above the houses and
streets of Canterbury and can be seen from almost anywhere
in the city. It is pictured here from Havelock Street.

Cathedral reflections.
The golden cathedral is reflected in one of
the old cobbled streets that wind through the city.

Westgate Towers.
Westgate Towers is one of the finest fortified gatehouses
to be built. It's seen here reflected in the River Stour.

Cathedral through the battlements.
This is one of the finest views to be had of the cathedral,
through the battlements on the top of Westgate Towers Museum.

View from Westgate Towers.
A wide angle view from the top of Westgate Towers Museum. This stunning view shows the beginning of St Peter's Street, the Marlowe Theatre on the left and Canterbury Cathedral.

Cathedral from University of Kent.
The University of Kent stands high on a hill and gives fantastic views of the Cathedral,
seen here rising majestically above the red roofs of the city.

Right: Blackfriars.
Blackfriars is the oldest Franciscan building in Britain and dates back to the thirteenth century. It is now The Dominican Youth and Community Centre.

Opposite: The Weavers' House.
The timbered gables of the Weavers' House overhang the River Stour. The ducking stool can be seen further up the river.

Right: Boat trips on the Stour.
Boat trips around the waterways of Canterbury take the visitor to the hidden secrets of the city and the unseen views from the River Stour.

15

The Miller's Arms.
Crossing the bridge into the Miller's Garden, The Miller's Arms can be
seen bathed in evening light and reflected in the River Stour.

St Martin's church.

St Martin's church is the oldest parish church in England and dates back to 597AD. St Augustine worshiped here whilst his abbey was being built. King Elthelbert gave the church to his Christian Queen, Bertha.

Window arch.
One of the ruined window arches of the abbey. The abbey
was destroyed around 1538 on the orders of King Henry VIII
when he decided to dissolve the monasteries of England.

Opposite: St Augustine's Abbey.
The abbey dates back to 597AD and was founded by St Augustine.
It's historically important as it marks the birth of Christianity in
England.   The site was originally used as a burial place for Anglo-
Saxon Kings of Kent. The ruins of St Augustine's Abbey form
part of the Canterbury World Heritage Site and are cared for
by English Heritage.

Lady Wootton's Garden.
These recent statues of King Ethelbert and his wife, Queen Bertha can be seen at the gardens. The statues depict
King Ethelbert greeting Queen Bertha on her return from prayers with the news of St Augustine's landing.

Queen Bertha.
The statue of Queen Bertha, the Christian Queen,
depicted returning from St Martin's church.

King Ethelbert.
King Ethelbert is depicted giving his Queen
the news that St Augustine had landed.

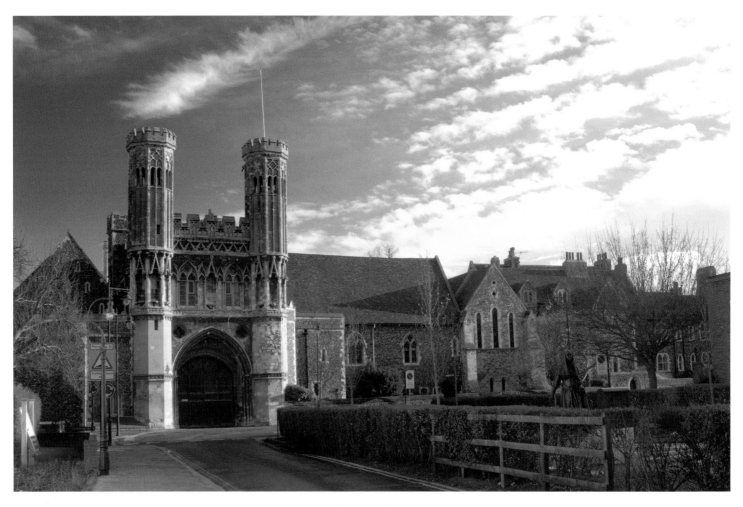

King's School.
King's School, Canterbury seen here from Lady Wootton's Garden. Some of the school's famous pupils include, dramatist Christopher Marlowe and William Harvey, King Charles I's physician who discovered the circulation of the blood.

St Peter's church.
St Peter's church dates from 1100AD and has
four ancient bells housed in its tower.

King's Gallery.
Subsidence maybe a problem with this house as it's at all
angles! The King's Gallery was formerly the Old King's
School shop and dates back to 1647.

Tower House from the River Stour.
Tower House was once part of Canterbury's city walls.
The current house is Victorian and dates from around 1850.
It is now the Lord Mayor's Office for official functions.

Opposite: Tower House.
This is the back view of Tower House from the gardens. The famous old
plane tree to the left of the building is believed to be 200 years old.

Canterbury Castle.
The ruins of Canterbury Castle date back to Norman times and lie close to the city wall on Castle Street. The castle replaced an earlier fortification at the nearby Dane John Gardens and was used as a prison in the twelfth century for the county of Kent.

Dane John Gardens.
The monument on top of the mound is to Alderman James Simmons who gave the gardens to the people of Canterbury. The hill is thought to be the sole survivor of several burial mounds in the area.

Café des Amis.
One of the multitude of restaurants to be found in Canterbury, catering for many different tastes. This one specializes in carefully prepared Mexican dishes.

Opposite: Cathedral from Howe Barracks.
The south side of the cathedral can be seen from the vantage point near Howe Barracks. The green netting around the cathedral shows where restoration work is being carried out.

Christchurch Gate.
This is the main entrance into the cathedral precincts. Chaucer's pilgrims would have probably entered here through the magnificent medieval gateway.

Statue of Christ over Christchurch Gate.
This is the modern statue of Christ over the medieval entrance of Christchurch Gate and can be seen from the market cross near Sun Street.

Cathedral from Abbot's Mill Gardens.
The view from Abbot's Mill Gardens of the Cathedral: as the sun goes down the late afternoon rays
give the towers a golden hue. The gardens are at their best in spring when the daffodils and blossom are out.

The Bell Harry Tower from the precincts.
The grand and intricate design and the scale of the cathedral can be
breathtaking. This is the view from the Christchurch Gate entrance.

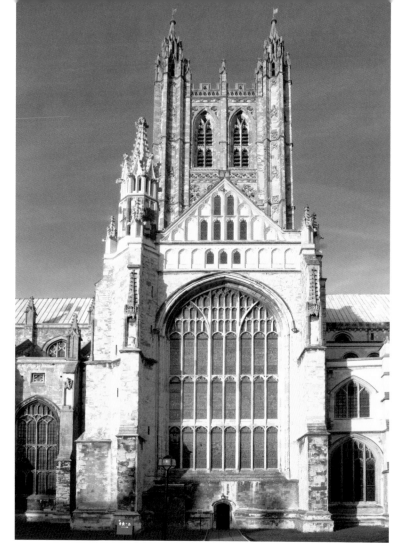

South West Transept, outside view.
The South West Transept, seen in the afternoon as the sun lights up this superb triumph of English architecture.

Opposite: Cathedral from Cathedral Shop.
The view of the west end of the cathedral in low afternoon light brings out the beautiful warm colours of the stone.

34

The South Aisle.
The beautiful Nave and Ailes date from
the fourteenth century and were designed
by the King's master mason, Henry
Yevele. They are a stunning example of
English Perpendicular Gothic
architecture.

Opposite: The Altar.
The Altar marks the central part of the
cathedral and is used by the Archbishop
of Canterbury during divine service.

Bell Harry Tower.
The Bell Harry Tower was extended in the late thirteenth century and is the structure we see today.
This picture is taken looking up from the floor of the cathedral.

The Martyrdom.
A striking modern sculpture marks the place where Thomas Becket
was murdered by King Henry the II's knights.

Great South Window.
This is one of the beautiful and magnificent stained glass windows of Canterbury Cathedral.
The cathedral has many stained glass windows which depict various stories and historical events.
This detail of the Great South Window shows figures from The Old Testament and dates from the twelfth century.

The Peace Window.
The Peace Window of 1956 depicts
Christ in Glory welcoming children of all
nations and is by Ervin Bossanyi.

Bosses.
This is one of the many bosses to be seen in the cathedral. The ceilings are an
intricate maze of colour and fine stonework, seen here in the cloisters.

The Black Prince.
The bronze figure of The Black Prince (Edward Plantagenet) lies on a magnificent tomb. The Black Prince lived from 1330 to 1376 and was the eldest son of King Edward III but died before his father and was never to be crowned king. He was famous for his military achievements.

King Henry IV and Joan of Navarre.
The tomb of King Henry IV and his wife Joan of Navarre lie on the north side of Trinity Chapel. Unusually for a king of England he was buried at Canterbury Cathedral and not Westminster Abbey. He lived from 1367–1413.

Bell Harry Tower from the Cloisters.
The Bell Harry Tower stands hundreds of feet high, here lit by the late evening winter sun. The intricate design of the cathedral stonework took years to complete.

St Dunstan's church.

St Dunstan's church is over a thousand years old and is linked with the Roper family. The head of Sir Thomas More was brought to the church by his daughter, Margaret, from the Tower of London. Sir Thomas More was beheaded whilst King Henry VIII was on the throne in 1535.

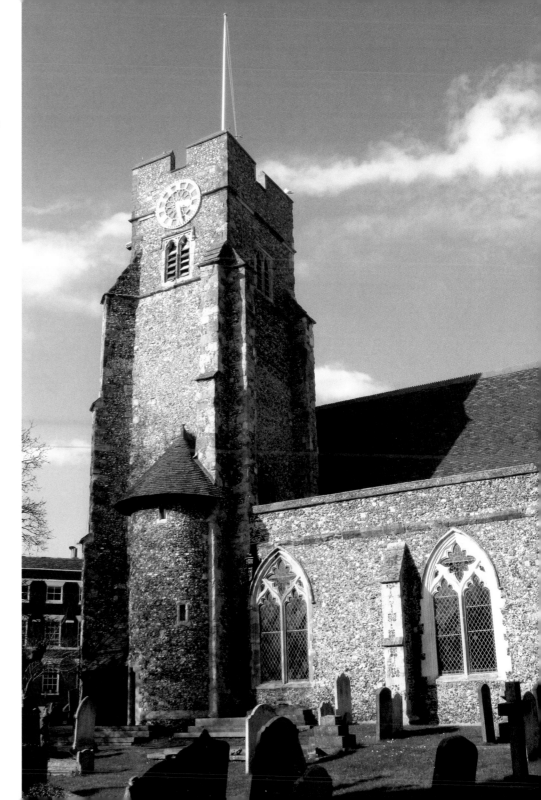

Framed house through archway. A medieval house seen through the ruins of the old city wall framed by magnolia trees. This archway leads to the River Stour near Westgate Gardens.

46

Daffodils by the River Stour.
Spring arrives at Westgate Gardens with a magnificent display of assorted daffodils lining the banks of the River Stour.

Westgate Towers and church.
Late March and the daffodils are at their best. This is the view of Westgate Towers from Westgate Grove.

Blackfriars and daffodils.
Clumps of brightly coloured
daffodils fill the foreground to
Blackfriars from the Abbot's Mill
Garden Garden's during early spring.

Blackfriars Rectory.
The rectory was built in 1237 and sits on an island in the River Stour. It belonged to the Dominicans who were known as Blackfriars because they wore black coats over their white habits.

Greyfriars.
Greyfriars is a thirteenth-century building and is all that remains of the original friary. It is the oldest Franciscan building in Britain and can be found in Greyfriars Gardens. The building spans the River Stour.

Fountain and trees.
This central fountain sits in the middle of Dane John Gardens
with an avenue of trees either side of the walkway

The fountain.
The fountain at Dane John Gardens marks
the central point of the walkway.

The War Memorial.
The War Memorial in Dane John Gardens commemorates the fallen soldiers of Kent during the Boer War (1899–1902). It was unveiled in May 1904 by Field Marshal The Rt. Hon. Earl Roberts.

The Buttermarket.

The Buttermarket is the small square just outside the main entrance of Christchurch Gate. The cross stands as a memorial to soldiers killed in The Great War. The Buttermarket is a hive of activity with its cafés, restaurants and street musicians.

St Andrew's United Reformed church.
This church is to be found on Watling Street, a short walk
down from Dane John Gardens. The church stands out as the
architecture is in stark contrast with the medieval Gothic style
of the cathedral.

Sun Hotel, Sun Street.
The Sun Hotel used to be known as The Little Inn and dates
from 1503; it was frequented by Charles Dickens as he
travelled through Kent.

Window reflections.
The cathedral pinnacles are captured reflected in the medieval leaded windows of a timbered building on Palace Street.

Opposite: Cathedral Pinnacles, Palace Street.
The cathedral pinnacles can be seen from almost anywhere in the city. The late afternoon
sun bathes the pinnacles in a golden light seen from Palace Street.

Westgate Towers from St Peter's Street.
Westgate Towers is the largest surviving city gate in England and dates back to the Norman times.
The Westgate marks the end of the London Road which pilgrims trod on their way to Canterbury.
The Towers were used as a prison from the fifteenth century. It is now a museum.

Tower House, front view.
Tower House is used as the Lord Mayor's Office. It was built around one of the 21 medieval strongholds
constructed to defend Canterbury's city wall. There has been a house on this site since the fifteenth century,
the current one being an early Victorian building, dating from around 1850.

Tower House and primulas.
At the back of Tower House is an extensive garden running alongside the River Stour. The gardens were given to Canterbury by Mr Stephen Williamson in June 1936. The Williamsons used to live in the house and the family has links with Canterbury going back 200 years.

The Ducking Stool.
The Ducking Stool can be seen from St Peter's Street just by the Old Weavers' House. The ducking stool was one of the ways used to find out if people were witches. The accused was dipped in the river to see if they would drown; if they survived it must be witchcraft. The surviving witch was then taken away and duly executed!!

Overleaf: Rooftops.
This view over the city can be seen from the battlements of Westgate Towers Museum. As the sun sinks on a winter's afternoon the last rays light up the cathedral, which rises high above the red rooftops.

Pilgrim's Hospital.

The Pilgrim's Hospital of St Thomas is located on St Peter's Street. The Hospital was founded around 1176, a number of years after Thomas Becket was killed. It was set up to cope with the huge influx of pilgrims coming to see his tomb. The Hospital was used in the old sense of the word, a place of hospitality.

Opposite: Westgate Towers and daffodils.

Spring is a wonderful time of year to visit Canterbury as all the gardens are full of bulbs. The daffodils at Westgate Gardens line the river bank of the Stour leading the eye through the picture towards the Towers.

Chilham square.
Chilham is a very picturesque village to the west of Canterbury and is often used in film and television dramas.
The village square dates from the middle ages and is a mix of half timbered buildings, shops and inns.
The twelfth century church was built for King Henry II.

Chilham Castle.
Chilham Castle dates from 1616 and is thought to have been designed by Inigo Jones, a favourite of
King James. The castle is privately owned and is not open to the public.

Taylors Hill, Chilham.
Taylors Hill is one of the roads that lead out of Chilham square. The Copper Kettle
Tea Rooms and Restaurant (on the right) is one of many fine eating places in the village.

Wingham church.
This is St Mary the Virgin church in Wingham village. The church spire can be seen
as you approach the village from the Ickham road. The church dates back to Norman times.

Cottages, Wingham.
A row of brick cottages with white picket fences and daffodils line the footpath on the High Street.

Wingham High Street.
Wingham lies on the ancient coast road from Richborough to London, now the A257. The village dates back to Roman times and has many thirteenth century buildings, including the church and the Red Lion Inn.

White cat, Patrixbourne.
Along one of the flint and brick walls of the village I spotted this stone white cat poised in one of the recesses. Such charming small details can easily be overlooked.

Patrixbourne church.
The church of St Mary serves this small community in the Canterbury district of Kent.

Timbered cottage.
Patrixbourne is a mix of old and new houses, this one being a timbered Tudor design.
Patrixbourne lies on the River Nailbourne, a small tributary of the Little Stour.

St Peter's, Bekesbourne.
Bekesbourne-with-Patrixbourne is a rural parish 4 miles south east of Canterbury. The place is renowned for hops and sunflowers. The church of St Peter dates back to medieval times. The famous Howlett's Zoo is quite close to Bekesbourne.

Oast Houses, Littlebourne.

These new oast houses lie on the River Nailbourne just by the green and have been built
in the style of the traditional Kentish oasts, which were used to dry hops.

The Green, Littlebourne.
Spring comes to Littlebourne as the daffodils open up to some welcome sunshine.

Ickham oasts.
A recent conversion has made these picturesque oast houses into homes. The village church can be seen to the left of the picture.

Water mill.
This water mill lies on the River Nailbourne on the road between Littlebourne and Wickhambreaux.

Ickham church.
St John the Evangelist church lies in the centre of the village, and dates from the thirteenth century. Next to the church are Ickham Barns, which are now well preserved thatched houses.

West Stourmouth.
This is the view of North Court Farm oast houses in the afternoon, viewed from Church Street outside the church of All Saints. The village of West Stourmouth is close to the Little Stour.

Chilham Water Mill.
Chilham Water Mill is maintained by Mid Kent Water and is fully restored. Mid Kent Fisheries
are also based here. Visitors are allowed to park and walk round the nature trail.

Pluck's Gutter.
The River Stour from the bridge at Pluck's Gutter, looking west over the marshes towards Sarre. The river splits in two at this point turning into the Little Stour and the Great Stour.

Pluck's Gutter.
Looking east down the River Stour which eventually ends up at Sandwich before heading out to sea.

Chillenden Windmill.
Chillenden Windmill is an open trestle post mill which dates from 1868. In November 2003 it blew over and was wrecked but fortunately it has now been fully restored to its former glory. It is seen here on a late summer evening in the middle of a cornfield.

Nuthatch.
The Nuthatch is one bird that can be found in the woods at Blean. They are often seen making their way down trees looking for food.

Left: Blean Woods.
This is Canterbury's ancient woodland and is the largest in Kent. The woods have many different species of trees and support a great deal of varied wildlife.

Kingfisher.
The kingfisher with its brightly coloured plumage of orange breast and iridescent blue wings is a frequent visitor to Stodmarsh. The habitat is ideal with big open pools of water and widespread reedbeds.

Overleaf: Stodmarsh.
Stodmarsh National Nature Reserve lies to the east of Canterbury and can be accessed via the village of Stodmarsh or from Grove Ferry. It has 241 hectares of wetland with extensive reedbeds. This is the place to visit if you want to see an abundance of wildfowl.

River Stour, Grove Ferry.
This is the view from the picnic site which is open all year. The late winter sunshine
lights up the River Stour creating beautiful reflections in the water.

North Downs, Folkestone.
The view looking towards Folkestone, encompasses the Channel Tunnel rail link. The Channel Tunnel is the second longest undersea tunnel in the world and came into service in 1994. It links Folkestone with Coquelles near Calais in France.

Royal Military Canal.
This is the bridge over the canal at West Hythe. The canal was built originally to defend Romney marshes from invasion by Napoleon and his French army. The canal stretches from Seabrook to Rye Harbour and was completed in 1809.

91

Southern Maid.

The Southern Maid is one of many steam engines that run along the Romney Hythe and Dymchurch Railway. This is the smallest public railway in the world and it runs from Hythe to Dungeness on 15 inch gauge tracks.

Right: Port Lympne Castle.

Lympne Castle sits high on a hill overlooking Romney Marshes. The castle has seen invaders come and go and was used as an observation post during the Second World War. Parts of the castle date back to the thirteenth century.

Bishopsbourne church.
A late afternoon picture of St Mary's church from Bourne Park. The author, Joseph Conrad used to live at Bishopsbourne in a house called 'Oswalds'. The village hall is named 'Conrad Hall' in his memory.

Bourne Park.
The footbridge over the stream is part of the Elham Valley Way which
goes from Canterbury all the way down to Hythe, a total of 22.5 miles.

Church at Chartham.
Chartham is a picturesque village with a large village green. The church of St Mary the Virgin
dates from the thirteenth century and has the oldest set of five bells in Kent.

The Great Stour.
The Great Stour runs round the outskirts of the village of Chartham and underneath the railway bridge. This is a delightfully tranquil spot by Riverside.

St Mary's church.
The last rays of the sun illuminate the side of St Mary's on Church Street, Sandwich. The church was built on one of the oldest church sites in the town. A seventh-century convent had been founded on the site previously.

Barge on the river.
The River Stour flows through Sandwich before making its way inland. Sandwich is one of the Cinque Ports which was an alliance between the ports of Dover, Hythe, New Romney and Hastings. It was created for military and trade purposes.

Pleasure boats.
During the winter months the River Stour at Sandwich is relatively quiet but in the summertime it is a hive of activity.

Rooftop view of Sandwich.
Sandwich is an old port and is one of the best preserved medieval towns in England. The Dutch came over during the sixteenth century and brought with them skills such as clay tile making which gives the rooftops their distinctive character. There are also many Dutch-gabled houses in the town. The church of St Peter is on the left of the picture and Sandwich Mill can be seen in the distance.

Overleaf: St Clement's view.
A wider view taken from the top of St Clement's church. The Norman church tower is the highest in Sandwich and served as a lookout post against raids by the Danes and French in times gone by. The tower survived an earthquake in 1578 but today it's in need of restoration.

The Abbot's Fireside.
The Abbot's Fireside restaurant was originally an inn called the Smithies built in 1451. The beautiful timbered building is on the High Street in Elham.

Cullings Hill.
Elham is a very charming village, with timbered medieval buildings and a Norman church. Cullings Hill is no exception and is one of the most photographed and painted by the visitor.

Elham.
Looking down at Elham village from the North Downs. Elham lies in the
valley of the same name and is an Area of Outstanding Natural Beauty.

Stelling Minnis Mill.
This is a grade one listed scenic smock mill which was built in 1866 and worked right up to 1970. The windmill is now owned by Kent County Council and is open to the public on certain days during the summer.

Stelling Minnis Mill.
Another view of the picturesque windmill which was fully restored in 2003.

Timbered house.
Petham is full of characterful cottages and semi-timbered buildings such as this one.
The church can be seen behind sitting on a hill overlooking the village.

Bluebells.
Spring arrives at a small woodland near Waddenhall Woods.

Opposite: Petham, Chequers Hill.
The road to Petham leads to the small charming village nestling
in the North Downs surrounded by arable farmland.

Lydden.
St Mary's church at Lydden surrounded by grazing animals. Lydden village is not far from Dover and is a rural delight.

Shepherdswell.
Enjoying a lunch time drink on the village green at Shepherdswell. The green is surrounded by a number of horse chestnut trees and a war memorial dedicated to the men who fell in The Great War.

Coldred.
Coldred sits nearly 400ft above sea level and is one of the highest villages in Kent.
The village pond was used for witch trials during the 1640s.

Overleaf: Ripple Windill.
Ripple Windmill from a rape field near Nelson's Seat. In the background is the coastal town of Deal.

Sun Hotel.

Returning from the surrounding countryside to the heart of Canterbury: people enjoying the sunny weather, eating and drinking outside the Sun Hotel between Guildhall and Sun Street.

Burgate.
Burgate leads to the Buttermarket and the entrance to the cathedral.

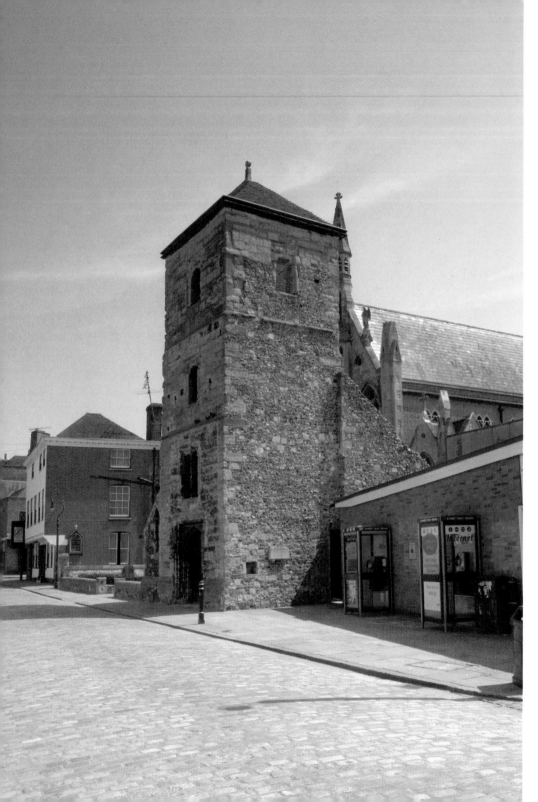

Church of St Mary Magdalene.
The church was founded before 1165 and the tower erected in 1503. This is all that remains of the church, the rest having been demolished in 1871. Richard Harris Barham was baptized here, author of *Ingoldsby Legends*.

The Old Buttermarket.

Canterbury is a much visited city and has a thriving café culture with people eating alfresco when the weather permits.

Little Italy.
Another eating establishment among the old timbered buildings near Kingsbridge on the High Street.

Boats for hire.
Summertime
and a wonderful
opportunity to enjoy
a gentle trip down
the river.

Punting down the river.
A very relaxing and peaceful way to see the city is by going on a boat tour departing from Westgate Towers.

Summer boat tours.
Boat trips are available from various locations. This one departs from
The Old Weavers' House and has room for four more people.

Palace Street.
Night time brings an atmosphere all of its own to the thriving city streets of Canterbury.

Blackfriars Street.
A evening view of the cathedral from Blackfriars Street, the main tower illuminated against the night sky.

123

The Old Weavers' House.
This must be one of the most atmospheric and historic restaurants in
Canterbury, beautifully lit up with warm welcoming lights.

Right: Cathedral at twilight.
The cathedral from Howe Barracks glows in the twilight
as the sun sinks over the horizon.

Overleaf: Sunset over Canterbury.
A wide view of a sunset over Canterbury city from the hill
up towards Howe Barracks.

River reflections, Riverside Court.
Riverside walks take the visitor around some of the most beautiful parts of
Canterbury as the River Stour flows through the city.

The River Stour.
Crossing the bridge at Westgate Gardens gives this stunning view of the river towards Westgate Towers.

Gate into Westgate Gardens.
This is one of the many old gates that lead into Westgate Gardens. The gates used to be part of the wall that surrounded the city.

Old gate house.
The crumbling remains of an old
gate house and bridge across the Stour from Westgate Grove.

Right: Tower House reflection.
The Tower House reflected in the river on a still
balmy summer evening.

Westgate Towers.
One of the main entrances to the city showing off its mellow coloured stone on a summer's evening.

**River reflection
from Westgate Towers.**
The River Stour flows round and
through the city before heading
off to Sandwich.

133

Blackfriars (summertime).
The rectory of Blackfriars from the calm
waters of the River Stour.

Miller's Arms and Mill Lane.
Another watering hole for pilgrims past and present to quench their thirst.

Restoration.
50 million pounds is needed to carry out major restoration works
to the cathedral to ensure its future for the next 500 years.

Opposite: Cathedral.
A parting view of the cathedral as one leaves the precincts through the shop.

Son of Man.
This statue of the Son of
Man is to be found on the east
side of the cathedral. The statue
is a work by David Mcfall RA.

Gargoyle.
Stonemasons carved grotesque faces and mythical creatures out of stone.
The gargoyles housed spouts to carry rainwater clear of the wall.

Cathedral Cloister columns.
Sunlight pours through the archways highlighting the
magnificent columns and throwing cool shadows across the floor.

Opposite: The Cloisters.
Cool calm and shady, the Cloisters provide
a covered walk around the quadrangle with majestic
vaulted ceilings decorated with elaborate painted bosses.

Kent vs Sussex.
A cricketer whacks the ball towards the boundary line as Kent
take on Sussex in the county championships.

Opposite: St Lawrence Cricket Ground.
The grounds are in Higham Park on Old Dover Road and are home
to Kent County Cricket. The club boasts 250 members and is said
to be one of the prettiest grounds in the country.

The Goods Shed.
Adjacent to the railway line, The Goods Shed is a farmers' market selling
local produce and provides an atmospheric venue for the stalls and restaurant.